IMAGES
of America

BALTIMORE'S
HISTORIC PARKS
AND GARDENS

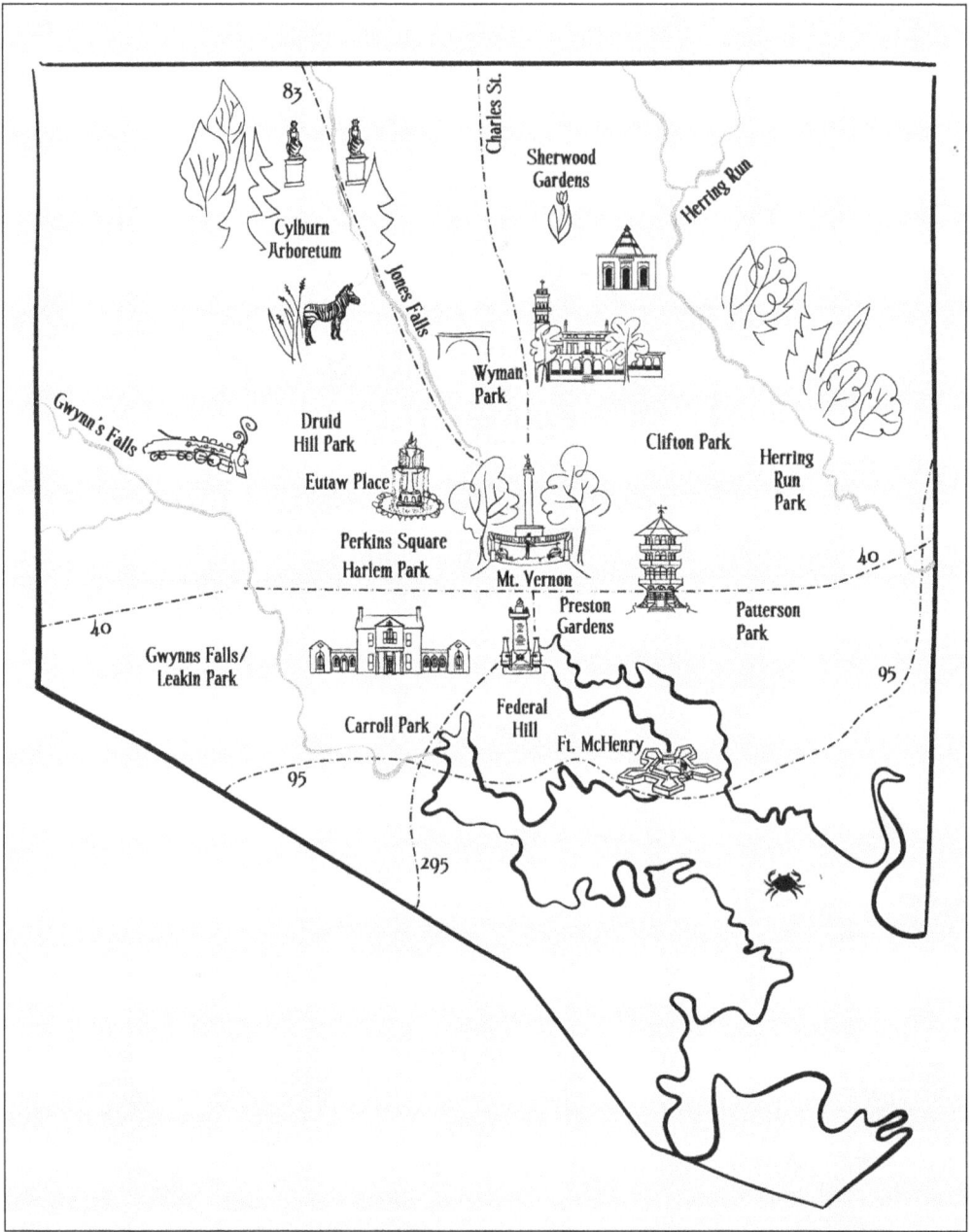

This original map by Peggy Fussell shows the locations of Baltimore's most prominent historic parks and gardens.

IMAGES
of America

BALTIMORE'S
HISTORIC PARKS
AND GARDENS

Eden Unger Bowditch
on behalf of the Cylburn Arboretum Association

ARCADIA
PUBLISHING

Published by Arcadia Publishing
Charleston, South Carolina

Library of Congress Catalog Card Number: 2004107283

For all general information contact Arcadia Publishing at:
Telephone 843-853-2070
Fax 843-853-0044
E-mail sales@arcadiapublishing.com
For customer service and orders:
Toll-Free 1-888-313-2665

Visit us on the Internet at www.arcadiapublishing.com

To Nate, Julius, Lyric, and Cyrus, my wonderful family—you make my life a garden.
And for the women who taught me so much about the soil and the magical things that come
from it—Elda Dixler Unger and Louise Jennison Bowditch, my gardening heroes.

The Mansion House at Cylburn Arboretum is seen here c. 1925.

CONTENTS

ACKNOWLEDGMENTS

I must first thank my husband, Nate, and my children, Julius, Lyric, and Cyrus, for their love and patience while I once again locked myself in the office and worked through too many dinners to complete a book project. Nate's unfailing ability to take care of us all and still help me with the photographs (taking many of the modern ones himself) and edits will never cease to amaze me. Lyric was a big help with the photo ordering, too.

I was very lucky to have so many of Baltimore's park champions eager and willing to donate their time and expertise. I extend my thanks to Enoch Pratt Free Library for the use of the majority of these wonderful photographs. As always, great and sincere appreciation goes to Jeff Korman, without whom this would never have happened. I cannot see how anyone could do a historic Baltimore project without him. Fellow Cylburn Arboretum Association board members Pat Draisey, Jane Baldwin, and Peggy Fussell were supportive and helped tremendously. Peggy's fabulous illustrations can be seen in the maps and drawings in these pages as well as in publications of the Brooklyn Botanical Garden, *The Baltimore Sun*, and Johns Hopkins University, to name a few. Peggy also provided some of the modern photography. Cylburn Arboretum Association executive director Susan Van Buren and Guy Hager from Parks and People organized and updated the list of organizations included as a resource for those interested in further participation. Several of Baltimore's most famous park activists were vital in this creation and lent their talents to the chapters on the "parks of their expertise." Tim Almaguer from Friends of Patterson Park provided several captions as well as photographs and the introduction to "Patterson Park." Sandy Sparks, president emeritus of Friends of Maryland's Olmsted Parks & Landscapes, Inc., provided the introduction for "Wyman Park." Myra Brosius and Trust for Public Land's Halle Van der Gaag both contributed to the introductions for "Carroll Park" and "Gwynns Falls/Leakin Park," respectively. Kate Blom provided the information and caption on Druid Hill Park's conservatory. Ranger Vincent J. Vaise from Fort McHenry also contributed photographs. Information about Sherwood Garden came from Bruce Barnet. Glenda Weber and Gerald Moudry allowed for the use of the historic postcards; Gerry Moudry's wonderful collection of postcards was an invaluable resource. Barry Kessler brought me his wonderful book *The Play Life of a City*. Also, it would have been impossible to complete this book without the help of Dorothee Heisenberg, Roz McCarthy, Stephanie Woodward, Sujata Massey, and Mary Bauer. Thanks to Jackie Salvagno for providing time with her presence. In her capable hands baby Cyrus enjoyed long afternoons of play while I was able to work on this project. Great appreciation and thanks go to Dan Unger for his editing skills. Also, thanks to Mary Roby, Abby Trauner, Fran Spero, Jennifer Morgan, Ann Draddy, Bill Vondrasek, Angela Rice, Melissa Grim, Jackie O'Regan, Harriet Felscher, June Behm, and so many others who provided vital bits of information or lent their time.

INTRODUCTION

I am not the only one who has fallen in love with Baltimore and its splendid green. Anyone who has been to Baltimore knows it is a green city. Under the direction of the Olmsted brothers and those who followed in their spirit, Baltimore has become an internationally award-winning city of gardens and parks. Over the years renovations and rehabilitation have, under the tension of extremely tight budgeting, helped many of the parks to maintain their beauty. We have lost some spaces and acquired others. It would have been impossible to note every green space since there seems to be some patch on every block. Baltimore has approximately 6,000 square acres of green space. There are some wonderful garden books showing off Baltimore's beautiful green, but there has yet to be a comprehensive volume of historic photos and backgrounds of at least most of these spaces. There are three main purposes for undertaking the project. The first is to give a brief history and show some historic and modern photographs of the parks throughout Baltimore. The second is to benefit Cylburn Arboretum Association. As a member of the board of directors, I am acutely aware of the financial needs of such an organization. All of the author's proceeds from this book will go to the arboretum. The third purpose is to offer a resource for anyone interested in contacting organizations involved with the parks and gardens. By providing contact information, I hope that anyone interested in becoming active in the parks and gardens of Baltimore will have a search made simple.

Most of all, enjoy this book. Take a step into the past and walk through these parks and gardens into the present and future. Love them, and they will give more than you can imagine.

Eden Unger Bowditch

FOREWORD

When Eden Unger Bowditch brought the proposal for this volume on Baltimore city parks to the Cylburn Arboretum Association, the Board received it with enthusiasm and complete support. The volume you are holding is the result of her unique approach to showcase many of the lovely park areas in the city.

Baltimore's parks show a great variety of features and facilities, ranging from the great natural areas of Leakin Park and Cylburn Arboretum to the actively used neighborhood parks such as Druid Hill Park and Patterson Park. Many city residents visit "their" local park on a regular basis, while other parks are not as well known as they deserve to be.

The author's longtime interest in and support of Cylburn Arboretum and her advocacy for Baltimore's beautiful city park system in general were central to the effort she brought to produce this guide. We expect that both city residents and visitors to Baltimore will be enjoying this review of the city's parks not only from the comfort of their homes with this volume in hand but also on foot to discover what the pictures and captions are all about. Thank you, Eden, for your fascinating guide to Baltimore's green public spaces.

Jane Baldwin
President, Cylburn Arboretum Association

FOREWORD

Dear Reader,

My first trip to Baltimore in early summer of 1996 included a visit to Cylburn Arboretum. Anne lived here, and we were dating. I was working at the Chicago Botanic Garden. She took me to Cylburn to show me that Baltimore had great public gardens, too. I was hooked on her, and she was trying to get me hooked on Baltimore.

It wasn't hard. Cylburn has a magnificent collection of trees and woody shrubs, thanks to the vision of the city's first chief horticulturist, Gerald Moudry. Cylburn also has an old-fashioned production greenhouse range, and I am a bit of a glass house fanatic, having cut my horticultural teeth in a similar facility in Chicago.

Imagine my excitement, then, when I first saw the Druid Hill Conservatory. I nearly burst when I heard the conservatory supervisor position was vacant! I moved to Baltimore, got the job, and got a wedding date.

Today I have the good fortune to have the best job in Baltimore as the new chief horticulturist in charge of both of these fine public gardens. The conservatory is set to reopen to the public after a $4.2 million renovation. The first floor of the mansion is now accessible to all and air-conditioned after its $700,000 renovation. In addition, the Cylburn Arboretum Association recently hired its first executive director, and together with the Department of Recreation and Parks, we are about to undergo Cylburn's first Master Planning process. It is a turning point for both of these two gardens.

What a great time then for this book, which highlights Cylburn, the conservatory, and all the other beautiful parks and gardens in Baltimore. Perusing its pages provides nearly as much pleasure as visiting the parks themselves.

After Mr. Moudry I use this signature . . .

Horticordially yours,
William Vondrasek
Chief Horticulturist
Baltimore Department of Recreation and Parks

This photograph of Eutaw Place was taken by the Baltimore Camera Club c. 1905. (Courtesy of Enoch Pratt Free Library.)

One

DRUID HILL PARK

Each park in Baltimore has its own fascinating history. Baltimore's first official park, however, was Druid Hill Park. Part of the land on which Druid Hill Park now stands was granted to Thomas Durbing (sometimes spelled "Durbin" or "Darbing") on June 30, 1688, by Charles, Lord Baltimore. He called it "Hab Nab a Venture." In 1703 Hab Nab and other pieces of property, with names such as The Level, Hap Hazzard, and Happy Go Lucky, came to be owned by carpenters, including Thomas Durbing's son, Christopher. The land was full of choice lumber. This was an era when carpenters had to find their own trees for wood. The young Durbing sold some of the land to another carpenter, John Eagleston, in 1703, while other acreage was sold to a carpenter named John Gardner in 1705. In 1716 Eagleston sold some of the land to Nicholas Rogers, a planter who came from an old English family. The name, then spelled "Rogier," was listed in William the Conqueror's Domesday Book, and this is the spelling Rogers often used in writing. The land owned by Rogers and the land owned by Gardner are the properties that now make up most of Druid Hill Park.

The land stayed in the Rogers family until 1860. Nicholas Rogers's daughter,

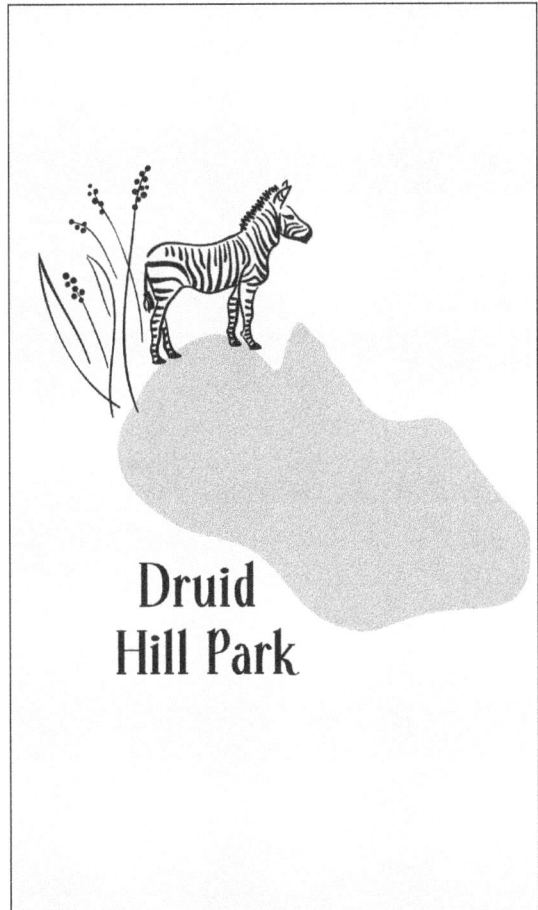

Druid
Hill Park

Eleanor, married George Buchanan, a young Scottish doctor, in the late 1720s. They had a son, Lloyd Buchanan, in 1729, the year that Baltimore Town was laid out. George Buchanan was one of the original seven commissioners. He purchased more land around his own and erected what could only be considered a castle on the site where the Mansion House now stands. He renamed the land Auchentorlie after his family's estate back in Scotland. Eleanor's youngest brother, also Nicholas Rogers, was wealthy in property as well. He had a son whom he, too, named Nicholas. It was this Nicholas who had a great influence on the overall landscape and, in all likelihood, the naming of Druid Hill Park.

Nicholas went to Scotland and finished his education in Glasgow, home of his Uncle George. At the time the news of the Revolution came from the colonies, he was living in Paris. It was then that a group of enthusiastic supporters of the cause were prepared to fight in aid of America's freedom. Among them was a "high-strung adventurer" named Gilbert Motier, better known as the Marquis de LaFayette. Rogers joined forces with the French army, and then Major Rogers sailed back and fought for his country. LaFayette's prestige shined on Rogers as his associate. He was made colonel and eased back into Baltimore life. Five years after his return, at age 25, he married Eleanor Buchanan, his cousin (as George Buchanan, at the age of 25 and five years after his arrival in Baltimore from Glasgow, married Eleanor Rogers).

Col. Nicholas Rogers was known to love landscape architecture and, in his studies in Glasgow, must have become enamored with the idea of oaks being the sentinels of the parks. He probably visited Stonehenge and read about the ancient Druids. It is supposed that Druid Hill came from these loves, and he supposedly planted trees according to their fall colors and beauty. The offspring of these trees most likely still thrive in the park, and the park's beauty as summer turns to autumn is matched only by Cylburn Arboretum. Rogers built a mansion (and rebuilt it after it was destroyed by fire) where the old castle once stood. This mansion stands today. Nicholas Rogers was known for his kindness as well as his aesthetic sense. His will, written in 1812, 10 years before his death, set free all of his slaves. The older slaves were employed, and the eldest, who could no longer work, was to be "taken care of to the last and be comfortably fed and clad—clad particularly because in want of that he will suffer seriously." He left his property to his children, the bulk to his only son, Lloyd Nicholas Rogers.

Lloyd Nicholas Rogers was supposed to have been a handsome young man, but as an old man he was a terror to children who crossed his path. He was not at all the man his father was and had no intention of freeing his slaves. The Rogers family estate came to an end with Lloyd Nicholas Rogers. He sold the land to the City in October 1860, and he died within a month. The park, along with the likes of Central Park in New York City, was part of an urban movement across the nation. With great European parks to guide the concept, green spaces were being created in cities to provide gardens and walking spaces for urban dwellers.

DRUID HILL PARK.

Druid Hill Park is known for its many attractions. Shown here is a drawing of the mansion house c. 1869. The mansion now houses the administration offices of the Baltimore Zoo. (Courtesy of Enoch Pratt Free Library.)

This is the mansion house c. 1934. (Courtesy of Enoch Pratt Free Library.)

These two photos show the duck pond c. 1907 (above) and c. 1900 (below). (Courtesy of Enoch Pratt Free Library.)

Fountains were a prominent feature in the Victorian-era Druid Hill Park. Many were decorative, and many were used freely by the city's residents as drinking venues. The water came from natural fresh springs that ran through the park. The fountains were closed when construction reportedly contaminated the water. (Courtesy of Enoch Pratt Free Library.)

This is Morris Fountain, c. 1900. (Courtesy of Enoch Pratt Free Library.)

15

Two young women pose at Crise Fountain, Druid Hill Park, c. 1890s. (Courtesy of Enoch Pratt Free Library.)

This water tower is a familiar site to all who know the park. Now seen from the freeway, the Lake Tower, here photographed on August 20, 1910, by the Baltimore Camera Club, is hard to miss. Built in 1870, it was a prime observation point for the then Chapman's Lake (subsequently called Druid Lake). It fell into disrepair and was closed to the public in the 1930s. (Courtesy of Enoch Pratt Free Library.)

The water tower is seen above the hill at this dedication ceremony of the Union Soldiers and Sailors monument on November 6, 1909. (Courtesy of Enoch Pratt Free Library.)

This is the nursery at the Madison Avenue entrance to the park c. 1938. (Courtesy of Enoch Pratt Free Library.)

This is a view from Garrett Bridge c. 1900. (Courtesy of Enoch Pratt Free Library.)

This is an artist's drawing c. 1870 of the state fish hatchery at Druid Hill Park. (Courtesy of Enoch Pratt Free Library.)

The fish house is shown here in 1907. (Courtesy of Enoch Pratt Free Library.)

This is the fish pond, *c.* 1870. (Courtesy of Enoch Pratt Free Library.)

This is the Buchanan Cemetery in 1938. The cemetery is still there, although it has succumbed to age. (Courtesy of Enoch Pratt Free Library.)

MARYLAND STAATS GEB.   PABELLON DE MARYLAND.   PAVILLON DU MARYLAND.

MARYLAND BUILDING.

This is a sketch of the Maryland Building at the Centennial in 1876. (Courtesy of Enoch Pratt Free Library.)

The boat lake in Druid Hill Park is filled with visitors on an afternoon in 1870. The zoo now surrounds the boat lake and, after years of being neglected, the lake has been brought back into use and once again is a splendid sight. (Courtesy of Enoch Pratt Free Library.)

The boat lake is seen through the trees, *c.* 1880. (Courtesy of Enoch Pratt Free Library.)

Here is Druid Lake in the winter, *c.* 1900. (Courtesy of Enoch Pratt Free Library.)

Eager skaters line up on New Years Day in 1895. (Courtesy of Enoch Pratt Free Library.)

There were only a few shepherds who ever worked at Druid Hill Park. The man who held the post the longest was George McCleary. He was a legendary figure, known to stay up all night with an ill or delivering ewe. Mr. McCleary ruled the flocks for many years. Shown here in 1910, he retired in 1926. (Courtesy of Enoch Pratt Free Library.)

Another shepherd and his dog watch the park *c.* 1880. (Courtesy of Enoch Pratt Free Library.)

Children play at Geyser Fountain, c. 1900. (Courtesy of Enoch Pratt Free Library.)

The stable yard is shown *c.* 1890. (Courtesy of Enoch Pratt Free Library.)

A member of the riding club is going for a ride on the park's bridle path, c. 1890. (Courtesy of Enoch Pratt Free Library.)

Although many paths became overgrown, beautiful roads and walkways still ribbon the park. Above is the Philosopher's Walk, and below is Crow's Nest Road, both c. 1900s. (Courtesy of Enoch Pratt Free Library.)

These are the dressing booths for one of the swimming pools, c. 1910. (Courtesy of Enoch Pratt Free Library.)

This tiny building once housed the city's aquarium but most recently was home to the zoo's reptile house. (Courtesy of Enoch Pratt Free Library.)

Land was retained for the conservatory in 1873. It was designed by prominent architect of the time George Aloysius Frederick (City Hall, Madison Avenue Arches) and was completed in 1888 at the height of the "crystal palace" movement. During the Civil War Druid Hill Park was called "Fort #5" and housed regiments from Maryland, Pennsylvania, Indiana, and New York. Artifacts—buttons, belt buckles, silverware—from these troops have been found on and around the grounds of the conservatory. In 1948 one of the most important Civil Rights demonstrations took place on the clay courts to the left of the Palm House. The Young Progressives of Maryland held a match with the Black Tennis Club of Baltimore to protest what were then the "whites only" courts. More than 500 people came to watch the match, the police were called, and the players were physically removed and arrested. The demonstrators lost their argument in municipal courts and appellate courts. The Maryland Supreme Court refused to hear the case. Despite this, the impact of this demonstration was very significant. Today, visitors can stroll through the newly planted Palm House that is lush with plants. The original Orchid Room has been restored, and the best and the brightest of its extensive orchid collection will soon be on display. The three display greenhouses have been excavated and refitted with all new systems, and they will feature plants from three distinct climates: desert, tropical, and Mediterranean (warm temperate). This is the Palm House exterior in a photo taken prior to 1920. (Courtesy of Enoch Pratt Free Library.)

This photo shows the Conservatory Palm House interior, prior to renovation. (Courtesy of Enoch Pratt Free Library.)

This is a postcard of the conservatory, *c.* 1900. (Courtesy of Gerald Moudry's postcard collection, Cylburn Arboretum.)

The conservatory is shown here with the new addition. The workmanship is spectacular, and the tremendous efforts made to match the style and feel of the Palm House show in the new building in 2004. (Photograph by Nathaniel Unger Bowditch.)

Workers clear leaves in autumn at Druid Hill Park, c. 1900. (Courtesy of Enoch Pratt Free Library.)

The Blacksmith repair shop is seen from the outside (above) and the inside (below) c. 1890. (Courtesy of Enoch Pratt Free Library.)

Druid Hill Park is home to the country's third-oldest zoological park. The zoo officially opened on April 7, 1876. Prior to that, deer roamed the park freely until the introduction of the automobile. After the deer were considered dangerous to have at large, they were confined to fenced-in areas in the park. In 1925 Mary Anne (seen here not long after her arrival) became the zoo's first elephant. She was purchased with the help of pennies collected by the city's children. Mary Anne died in 1941. In addition to its rich history, the zoo is a prime venue today. It was voted top children's zoo in the United States in 1994. (Courtesy of Enoch Pratt Free Library.)

These elk are among the earliest official residents, c. 1900. (Courtesy of Enoch Pratt Free Library.)

The camels were also early members of the zoo family, c. 1900. (Courtesy of Enoch Pratt Free Library.)

The sea lions were also an attraction at the zoo in its early days. A mother and cub arrived in 1884. Sadly, the cub died almost immediately, and the mother died three years later. This photo of the sea lion pond was taken c. 1895 with a new population of animals. Sea lions are still a favorite. The deer (below) are from 1930. (Both courtesy of Enoch Pratt Free Library.)

Druid Hill Park was famous for its multiracial visitors. Unfortunately, it also suffered under the "separate but equal" era of segregation, during which there were separate swimming pools, tennis courts, and other facilities available for either blacks or whites. Without question, these facilities were anything but equal. Protests and illegally integrated tennis matches brought an end to this unjust practice but not for many years. Although there is documentation showing black and white families enjoying Baltimore's parks together in 1850, Frederick Douglass was denied permission to speak in Druid Hill Park in 1865. Prior to the 1890s Baltimore was known to have very "fluid" race relations. Segregation and racial tensions made using public parks less comfortable for African-American families. Still, as we see by these young tennis players, above, the facilities were still in use. Below is a baseball game, c. 1931. (Both courtesy of Enoch Pratt Free Library.)

This is a view of the Druid Hills Mansion House in 2004. (Photo by Nathaniel Unger Bowditch.)

Two

CYLBURN ARBORETUM

Cylburn Arboretum is often considered the "Green Heart of Baltimore." The Cylburn Arboretum Association celebrates its 50th anniversary in the year 2004. The history of the grounds and gardens goes back much further. The mansion and the property that surrounds it were the possession of Baltimore businessman Jesse Tyson, who began building the mansion in 1863. The house was to be home to Tyson and his mother. Tyson married the young and beautiful Edyth Johns in 1888 (Johns was 19 and Tyson was 60), and the mansion became their home until Tyson died in 1906. His widow married Maj. Bruce Cotton four years later, and they lived in the mansion until her death in 1942. It was then that the house went up for auction. The City of Baltimore bought the property for $42,300 (approximately $235 per acre), which was a considerable deal, even then, for it had been valued at $92,000.

The property was then used by the Department of Public Welfare as the Home for Neglected Children. In 1954 the Board of Recreation and Parks founded Cylburn Wildflower Preserve and Garden Center on the property. Trails and gardens were

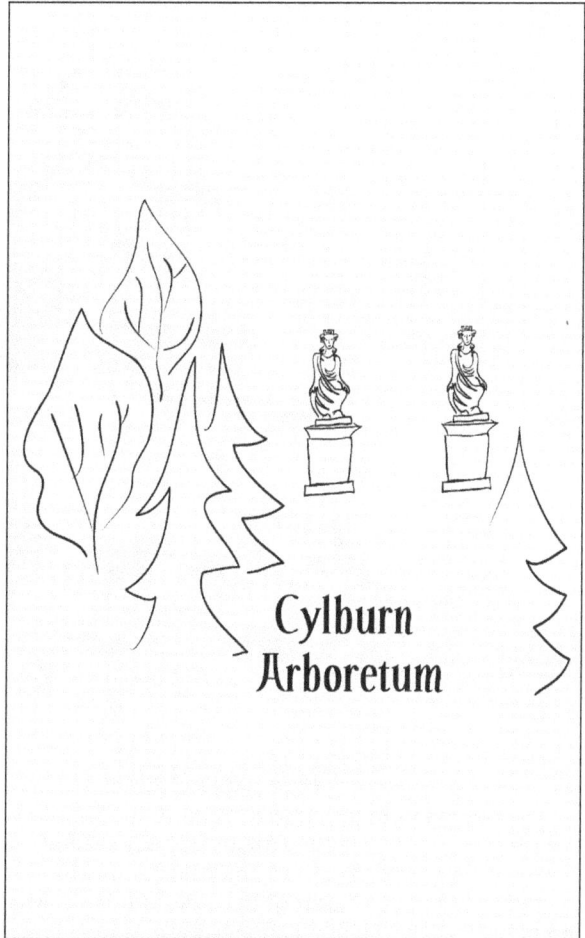

Cylburn
Arboretum

developed, as well as a center for horticulture, all by the work of volunteers. In 1982 the Preserve became Cylburn Arboretum, and the volunteer organization was named Cylburn Arboretum Association, Inc. The offices of Cylburn Arboretum Association and the Horticulture Division of Baltimore City's Department of Recreation and Parks are both housed in the mansion. On the approximately 207 acres are wildlife trails, formal gardens, and myriad trees, both exotic and domestic.

This is the Tyson Mansion as it stood in its glorious early days. The bottom floor now houses the offices of the Cylburn Arboretum Association. The upper floors house the Department of Horticulture and, formerly, the Museum of the Birds of Maryland. The mansion was built of gneiss from Tyson's own quarries at Bare Hills, Maryland. Many of the fine details are still intact throughout the house. (Courtesy of Enoch Pratt Free Library.)

Above is the interior front entrance hall as it was c. 1800. Tapestries later replaced the wallpaper shown here after Edyth Johns became mistress. Below is an interior view with the downstairs drawing room displayed in full regalia. (Both courtesy of Enoch Pratt Free Library.)

Above, the mansion is pictured from the northeast. Below, the mansion is seen from the southwest. Both photos were taken *c.* 1890s. (Courtesy of Enoch Pratt Free Library.)

This view is from the mansion's cupola, prior to 1900 (possibly taken in the 1880s). (Courtesy of Enoch Pratt Free Library.)

Two views of the grounds were taken *c.* 1900. (Courtesy of Enoch Pratt Free Library.)

Above, the lily pond is shown as it was at the turn of the last century. The pond is no longer there. Below, the formal gardens are pictured c. 1890. (Courtesy of Enoch Pratt Free Library.)

This is the old Tyson private train stop. The little bungalow, according to then-local resident Vernon C. Smith, was "painted beige with red trim, looking like something Walt Disney might have built." This stop went off line c. 1920.

A modern view shows the Mansion House in 2002. (Photo by P. Draisey.)

A view of one of the wilderness trails is pictured above in 2003; the formal gardens are seen below in 2003. (Photos by P. Draisey.)

The Lady Baltimore statue overlooks the Formal Garden. The Lady Baltimore statue is one of two that overlook the Formal Garden at the arboretum. It is one of the four statues designed by Herman Henning in the late 1800s that originally sat at the entrances to the St. Paul Street Bridge, which spans the Jones Falls. The statues were removed in the late 1950s. One is in the Mt. Royal Terrace Gardens in Reservoir Hill. Another was sent to Ireland in 1974 to County Longford near Bal (or Baille) Tighe More Lane, which was once part of George Calvert's baronial lands. (Photo by P. Draisey.)

This is the mansion from the northeast side in 2003. (Photo by P. Draisey.)

The lion statues are on the east side of the mansion. A few of the award-winning maples can be seen in the background. (Photo by P. Draisey.)

This trail is blanketed in autumn foliage. (Photo by P. Draisey.)

The mansion house is glowing in winter 2003. (Photo by P. Draisey.)

Volunteer Brigitte Harper and Cylburn Arboretum Association president Jane Baldwin are at work in the greenhouse. (Photo by P. Draisey.)

The Shady Garden is shown here in 2003. (Photo by P. Draisey.)

This is a view from beneath the canopy of the Japanese maple. The cluster near the mansion creates a magical pixie land that is enchanting to all who venture within. The award-winning maples collection at Cylburn is quite extensive. (Photo by P. Draisey.)

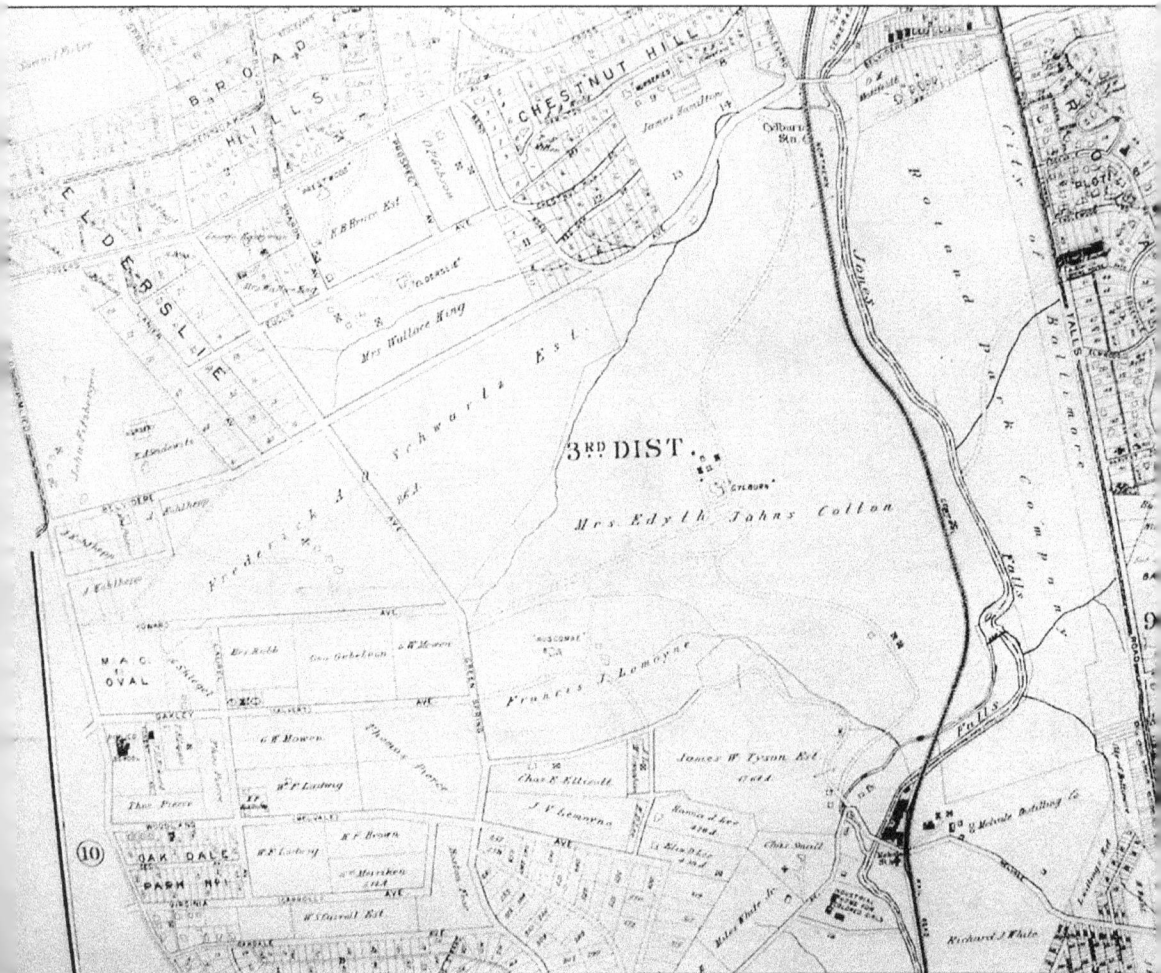

This map from 1915 shows the location of the Tyson property. An interesting fact to note is that adjacent to the property is the Frederick A.O. Shwartz (i.e. F.A.O. Schwartz) Estate. (Courtesy of Enoch Pratt Free Library.)

Three

HERRING RUN

Herring Run was also part of the
Olmsted vision. In their 1904 plan
for the city, the Olmsted brothers
recommended acquiring land along
the stream. Land for the park was
acquired in the 1920s, including
over 46 acres donated in 1926 by
the Garrett family. Herring Run
Watershed Association has been
very active in planting trees, helping
to restore the stream, and initiating
other positive ecological action.

**Herring
Run
Park**

Children get a drink from Hall's Spring, c. 1910. (Courtesy of Enoch Pratt Free Library.)

The old stone mill shown in this 1907 photo once stood on the land.

This stream runs through the park, *c.* 1910. (Courtesy of Enoch Pratt Free Library.)

This photo of a high rocky bank was taken in 1912. (Courtesy of Enoch Pratt Free Library.)

This was called "Copperhead Retreat" since it was a favorite breeding ground for copperhead snakes, 1907. (Courtesy of Enoch Pratt Free Library.)

The 1935 Baltimore Emergency Relief Commission begins work. (Courtesy of Enoch Pratt Free Library.)

This bridge was under construction by the Baltimore Emergency Relief Commission, as seen in 1935. (Courtesy of Enoch Pratt Free Library.)

Four

CLIFTON PARK

Clifton Park was once the country estate of Johns Hopkins. The property was part of his university endowment. Hopkins's intention was that Clifton be used as the site for the university and hospital he was to establish in his name. Clifton, the name of the estate, was deemed too far from the center of the city, and Homewood was chosen instead for the site of the university. The land and mansion house were sold by his executors to Baltimore City in 1894 for approximately $1 million. Like many great parks that had once been estates, Clifton's mansion house still stands.

Clifton Park

Visitors enjoy an afternoon in the park on the lawn of the mansion house, 1900. (Courtesy of Enoch Pratt Free Library.)

This portrait of Johns Hopkins (1795–1873) belongs to the Johns Hopkins University. (Courtesy of Enoch Pratt Free Library.)

The same visitors as on the previous page are seated near the carriage arch on the side of the mansion, 1900. (Both courtesy of Enoch Pratt Free Library.)

This photo shows the original greenhouses built by Hopkins, c. 1900.

Gardeners work in the flower bed, *c.* 1900. (Courtesy of Enoch Pratt Free Library.)

The gardener's house at Clifton is shown here *c.* 1890s. (Courtesy of Enoch Pratt Free Library.)

The lily pond is pictured as it was *c*. 1900s. (Courtesy of Enoch Pratt Free Library.)

The lawn mower, *c*. 1890s, had quite a task. (Courtesy of Enoch Pratt Free Library.)

The baseball diamond at Clifton Park is full of young players, *c.* 1910. (Courtesy of Enoch Pratt Free Library.)

Clifton Park golf course is shown here *c.* 1950s. Golf is a major activity at Clifton Park these days. Many know the park as home to one of Baltimore's popular public golf courses. (Courtesy of Enoch Pratt Free Library.)

Five

PATTERSON PARK

Urban parks are so many things to so many people. Often they afford the opportunity for spiritual sanctuary amongst the trees and lulling vistas, but often they are simply a safe place away from the harsh dirge of city streets and the oppression of bricks and mortar. They are places where friends and family meet and stroll to talk about the day; where children learn how to play freely in the grass, and where communities come together to celebrate.

These were the original tenets of landscape architects like Frederick Law Olmsted, whose philosophy had direct influence on the founders of Baltimore's park system. In the 1860s John H.B. Latrobe saw to the creation of Baltimore's park system, envisioning urban green ways that would cleanse people's hearts, minds, and lungs. During the height of Baltimore's industrial and commercial era and burgeoning population, these urban parks would bring to mind the pastoral views seen in Thomas Cole paintings and read about in Emersonian prose. Simply put, parks were somewhere to relax and leave the daily stress behind. This same legacy lives today.

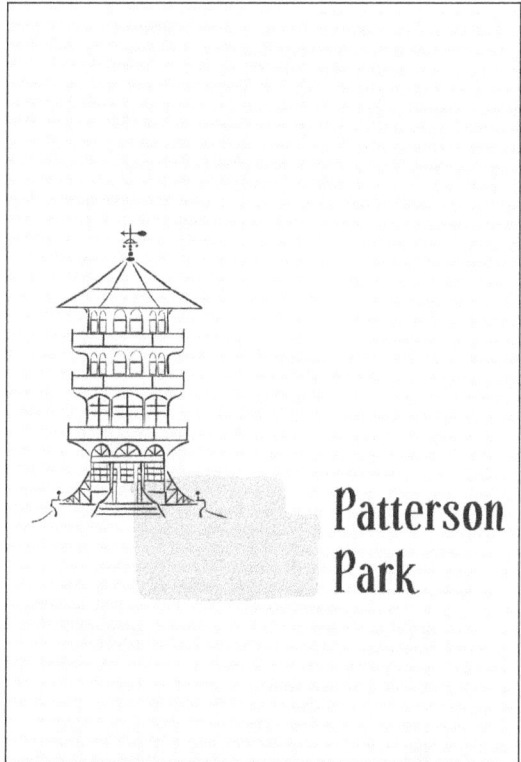

Patterson
Park

Established as a "Public Walk" by William Patterson in 1827, the original six acres quickly became a celebrated promenade. This location was also the famous "Rodger's Bastion" upon Hampstead Hill. Here in September 1814, as Fort McHenry was being bombarded, 12,000 American troops, many Baltimore volunteer militia, created an earthworks to repulse the advancing British wishing to burn Baltimore. The British retreated, and soon this site became a historical vista, now where the Pagoda stands.

William Patterson died in 1835, leaving much of the surrounding land to his heirs. Through the years Baltimore City annexed and bought this property as extensions to the original six-acre Public Walk, and in 1853 Patterson Park became an official public park in Baltimore City, one of the first in the United States.

The ideas of Frederick Law Olmsted and Andrew Jackson Downing became common philosophy for urban parks, and in the late 1850s plans for Patterson Park's design were being developed to utilize many of these same ideas and themes. As these plans were ready to come to fruition, the Civil War erupted, and many of Baltimore's parks and estates became encampments for Union troops. Patterson Park was no exception, and in 1861 it became home to many Union troops from New York, Wisconsin, and Maine. Later Camp Washburn was erected as a 1,000-bed surgical hospital.

After the union encampment left Patterson Park in 1864, the former plans were set into action, and many new promenades, facilities, and architectural elements were constructed: Marble Fountain, Superintendent's Residence, maintenance buildings, and Boat Lake. As Patterson Park grew in acreage many new attractions were built to accommodate needs and increased user-ship in the park. During the late 19th century new exploration to exotic lands brought new ideas, motifs, and floral specimens, and many of the park's architectural additions are influenced by this new knowledge, such as the conservatory and the Pagoda.

Today many of these same features and buildings are being restored to their original grandeur. Now grown to 137 acres, Patterson Park is seeing a renaissance. For generations many friends and families have enjoyed the park. Patterson Park had gone through an era of decline; however, the community, working with The Baltimore City Recreation and Parks, created a master plan for the park's redevelopment and has begun to implement these renovation projects.

Patterson Park has once again become a place for families, friends, and visitors to enjoy city life in a green environment. That is why they called Patterson Park "Baltimore's Best Backyard!"

Tim Almaguer, Project Coordinator, Friends of Patterson Park
(Tim also provided captions for the photos noted "Courtesy of the Friends of Patterson Park.")

Women keep the sun away with parasols at Mayday at Patterson Park, c. 1900. (Courtesy of Enoch Pratt Free Library.)

This is an illustration of Patterson Park from 1864 originally published in *Frank Leslie's Illustrated Newspaper*. (Courtesy of Enoch Pratt Free Library.)

This postcard of the boat lake dates *c.* 1900. What started as a grading accident in the 1860s became a focal point to Patterson Park. The manmade lake was created in 1864. It was expanded in 1875 to accommodate skating and became an incredibly popular skating venue. The shelter at the boat landing was added in 1884. Today the lake contains a wetland habitat for fish, turtles, and waterfowl. (Courtesy of Gerald Moudry's postcard collection, Cylburn Arboretum.)

NIGHT SCENE IN PATTERSON PARK.

This 1870 engraving shows the Patterson Park Boat Lake at night. (Courtesy of Enoch Pratt Free Library.)

This shows one of the first baseball games of the 1937 season for the Baltimore Amateur League. (Courtesy of Enoch Pratt Free Library.)

This postcard shows the conservatory at Patterson Park, c. 1900. The conservatory once stood where the children's playground is now. The intense interest that followed the publication of Darwin's *Origin of Species* and the subsequent surge in research and the acquisition of specimens are considered to be the impetus for the creation of the four conservatories in Baltimore. The "Gilded Age" architecture (as seen in the Palm House at Druid Hill Park) was the style in which Lord and Burdham built Patterson Park's conservatory in 1876. Sadly, the original wooden structure began to deteriorate in 1905 and was eventually razed in 1948. Baltimore City once had four conservatories; Patterson Park, Lake Clifton, Carroll Park, and, of course, Druid Hill, which still remains. (Courtesy of Gerald Moudry's postcard collection, Cylburn Arboretum.)

In the early 1900s small row boats covered the lake, some with young lovers, others with vacationers and local families. (Courtesy of The Friends of Patterson Park.)

Built in the 1920s, this huge music hall was constructed mostly of wood and had a wrap-around porch. The pavilion was the scene of many live musical concerts and dances. Unfortunately, in 1972 this pavilion succumbed to an arsonist's fire and had to be razed. (Courtesy of The Friends of Patterson Park.)

76

The Patterson Park pool and bathhouse, built at the turn of the 20th century, was designed and conceived by the famous Olmsted brothers. The new public concern for health and hygiene in the ever-growing urban environment of the early 1900s resulted in the inclusion of public pools and baths in municipal parks. (Courtesy of The Friends of Patterson Park.)

The Superintendent's House was built in 1866 by George A. Frederick (the architect of Baltimore's City Hall). This was the first park building in Patterson Park and was home to the park's superintendent until the 1970s. The first park element was the nearby marble fountain built in 1865, shortly after the Civil War encampment left the park. (Courtesy of The Friends of Patterson Park.)

A floral urn sits at the base of the Pagoda during the turn of the 20th century. The unusual appearance of the Pagoda is due to the use of exotic motifs in park architecture during the Gilded Age, as the builders often used Islamic and Asian themes to stylize park facilities. The Pagoda stands 60 feet tall and is adorned with stained-glass panels and hand-crafted woodwork. (Courtesy of The Friends of Patterson Park.)

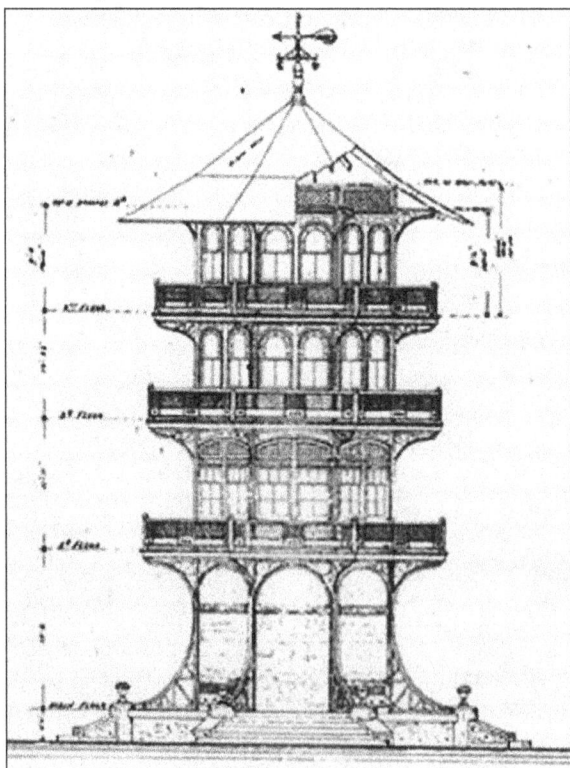

This is a blueprint of Patterson Park Observatory Pagoda, built in 1891 by Charles Latrobe. It sits on the site of Rodger's Bastion. Made famous for its redoubts against the approaching British during the Battle for Baltimore September 1814, this famous earthwork still exists. (Courtesy of The Friends of Patterson Park.)

The Pagoda was photographed
c. 1900. (Courtesy of The Friends of
Patterson Park.)

This c. 1910 picture shows how the Pagoda
was used by park police. (Courtesy of The
Friends of Patterson Park.)

Designed by Charles Latrobe and built in 1893 as a community center, the "Casino" later served as headquarters for Baltimore City Recreation and Parks, the home of the deputy superintendent, and a venue for dances and local events. (Courtesy of The Friends of Patterson Park.)

This postcard shows the Patterson Park Conservatory, c. 1900. (Courtesy of The Friends of Patterson Park.)

This postcard shows another view of the conservatory. (Courtesy of The Friends of Patterson Park.)

The main promenade of Patterson Park was lined with huge floral urns and paved with blocks. Families could be seen strolling along this walk and picnicking under the trees that lined the promenade. Along this path were the octagonal rain shelter and the conservatory. (Courtesy of The Friends of Patterson Park.)

The marble fountain is pictured in action at the entrance to the park. (Photograph by Nathaniel Unger Bowditch.)

A view of boat lake was taken in 2004. (Photograph by Nathaniel Unger Bowditch.)

Six

FEDERAL HILL

This park was named Federal Hill because of its connection to the Maryland ratification of the Constitution. After a 1779 celebration in the park, the name was changed from John Smith Hill to Federal Hill. The city did not officially purchase Federal Hill until 1875. Because of the numerous tunnels, the foundation of the park has had to undergo renovations in hopes of preventing future cave-ins. Federal Hill served as a stronghold during the Civil War. The view is quite extraordinary, and modern facilities (paving, benches, playground) make this historic park a great Baltimore site. The name Federal Hill now refers to the surrounding neighborhood as well as the park.

Federal Hill

FORT FEDERAL HILL, BALTIMORE, Md.

This drawing shows the outbreak of the Civil War in May 1861. It was in the middle of the month that Union general Benjamin F. Butler occupied and fortified Federal Hill. The 5th Regiment Massachusetts Volunteers are seen here at Fort Federal Hill as they garrisoned the fort. (Courtesy of Enoch Pratt Free Library.)

samuel Burrill's House.   Eighth Regiment Flagstaff.   Marine Observatory.

This woodcut from *Frank Leslie's Illustrated Newspaper* shows crowds standing at Johnson and Hughes Streets, May 18, 1861. (Courtesy of Enoch Pratt Free Library.)

FROM THE EAST.

INTERIOR

FROM THE SOUTH.

This is a lithograph by E. Sachse & Co., 1862. (Courtesy of Enoch Pratt Free Library.)

The images above and below depict Federal Hill during the Civil War. (Courtesy of Enoch Pratt Free Library.)

The observatory at Federal Hill was erected in 1797 and, sadly, razed in 1898. (Courtesy of Enoch Pratt Free Library.)

Federal Hill Park,   BALTIMORE, M

This illustrated postcard shows Federal Hill Park, *c.* 1900. (Courtesy of Gerald Moudry's postcard collection, Cylburn Arboretum.)

This view shows improvements, "dressing the slope," by the Works Progress Administration (WPA), *c.* 1935.

Sixty WPA employees had worked to clean up the park. The steps and reinforcement of the terrace, as well as smoothing the slopes and putting concrete in the paths instead of mud and dirt, was completed by the team. (Courtesy of Enoch Pratt Free Library.)

In this Civil War–era photo the guns are trained on Baltimore. (Courtesy of Enoch Pratt Free Library.)

Seven

FORT MCHENRY

Considered the birthplace of the national anthem (Francis Scott Key wrote the poem aboard a ship in the harbor below), Fort McHenry has a military history going back to 1776, when its strategic position at the end of the peninsula made it an ideal defense post. At the time it was called "Whetstone Point," a name still associated with the area, although Locust Point is more commonly used. The star-shaped fort was named in 1798 after James McHenry, who served as secretary of war under George Washington. The full name of the park is Fort McHenry National Monument and Historic Shrine It has undergone many expansions and renovations, doubling its land in the 1800s. Although it did not officially become a park until 1933, transferring control from the War Department to the Department of Interior, National Park Service, it was used as a park for a short time after 1912

until World War I. Many archeological digs have uncovered a plethora of military and other artifacts. The park museum has an exhibit of some of these artifacts. Fort McHenry was used in World War II as a U.S. Coast Guard Station but has remained a venue for those interested in military history. In fact, history is quite alive at Fort McHenry. On summer evenings, the Fort McHenry Guard is "on duty" with cannon demonstrations, drills, and civilian activities.

This photo taken c. 1906 at Fort McHenry shows cannons from the War of 1812 and, in the background, the stone chapel, which was razed. (Courtesy of Enoch Pratt Free Library.)

Fort McHenry is seen at dawn in 1939.

The Fort McHenry Guard conducts artillery firings on selected weekends during the summer season, 1993. (Courtesy of National Park Service, Fort McHenry NM&HS.)

Volunteers portray the citizens of Baltimore on summer weekends. Here, a "merchant" sells period items to visitors at Fort McHenry, 1993. (Courtesy of National Park Service, Fort McHenry NM&HS.)

Eight

CARROLL PARK

Mount Clare, the mansion still standing in what is now Carroll Park, was built in early 1754 by Dr. Charles Carroll and became the home of his son, Charles Carroll, the barrister. In its earliest days Mt. Clare was noted for its beautiful terraced gardens and Margaret Tilghman Carroll's fabulous citrus trees, some of which were given as gifts to George Washington. The Tokay grapes the Carrolls grew were reported to make excellent wine. Also, pineapples were a specialty of Mrs. Carroll's greenhouse. The Carrolls were very committed to their garden and had hired gardeners (including one exasperating convict who apparently escaped with a pilfered treatise on pineapples) to help maintain the beautiful estate. They had a library that contained numerous gardening books. The Carrolls' dedication to their terraced garden, meticulously maintained in the style of ancient Rome, showed that their love of the aesthetic, combined with extensive research, created a memorable union.

Carroll Park

After the Civil War, the Carroll family no longer occupied the mansion or the estate. They leased it to various tenants until it was purchased by the city in 1890 and designs were laid out by the Baltimore Park Commissioners in 1898. It then became Carroll Park. Carroll Park is Baltimore's third country landscape park, after Druid Hill and Patterson Parks, and is an example of integrating two eras in park design—the country landscape parks of the 19th century and athletics facilities popular in the 20th century. Located in southwest Baltimore, Carroll Park is 117 acres. Mount Carroll includes the oldest of two Federal-style mansions still standing in Baltimore City. The mansion is furnished accurate to the period, and, remarkably, most furnishings were owned by the Carroll family. The mansion is a National Landmark, and the park is eligible for listing on the National Register of Historic Places.

As the park continued to grow in acreage, the nationally acclaimed Olmsted brothers were hired to help respond to the growing interest in playgrounds and athletic recreation. The Olmsteds' plan expanded on the original design and helped to define the landscape character as it still exists today, integrating new recreational facilities including ball fields, tennis courts, a running track, and playground. While the basic form remains from the 19th-century park, the original park contained an impressive array of trees and formal gardens—including a conservatory—which are no longer there.

In recent years, the Baltimore City Department of Recreation and Parks rehabilitated the park, guided by the recommendations of A Master Plan for Carroll Park, 2001. The plan establishes policy for preserving the historic landscape while rehabilitating the park to serve the needs of the community.

Today Carroll Park boasts an assortment of new athletic fields—home to the Carroll Park Little League—a neighborhood playground, a skateboard park, and a nine-hole golf course.

—with Myra Brosius

This is a view of Mount Clare, approaching from Washington Boulevard through the grounds of Carroll Park, 1936. (Courtesy of Enoch Pratt Free Library.)

In the 1970s many of the larger trees and other flora were removed. Here, in 1936, we see three Scotch elms, reported to have been 180 years old then. The largest of these trees was said to be 53.5 inches in diameter. (Courtesy of Enoch Pratt Free Library.)

Pictured above is Mount Clare c. 1910. (Courtesy of Enoch Pratt Free Library.)

This is another beautiful view of the mansion, 1937. (Courtesy of Enoch Pratt Free Library.)

These photos show the interior of the mansion, with furniture said to have been purchased by Carroll in 1765. (Courtesy of Enoch Pratt Free Library.)

These photographs show the rose trellis in the Mount Clare garden c. 1910. (Courtesy of Enoch Pratt Free Library.)

A stone freshwater grotto, to the northeast of the mansion, is now dry. The feature was likely added in the late 1890s as the park was first developed by the Baltimore Park Commission. (Photo by Peggy Fussell; caption by Myra Brosius.)

Nine

MT. VERNON

The Washington Monument, at the center of Mt. Vernon Place, was originally going to be erected in the heart of Baltimore City. It was 1809, and a group of prominent Baltimoreans wanted to erect a monument to honor George Washington, who had died 10 years earlier. The site was selected. It would occupy the place where the old courthouse was being razed on Calvert Street between Fayette and Lexington. In 1815, when the winner of the design competition was revealed, the neighbors were up in arms. The design was a massive column by Robert Mills, and the homeowners around where it was to stand were sure that it would fall on their homes or at least be struck by lightening. Baltimore Revolutionary hero Col. John Eager Howard offered a portion of his vast estate, Belvidere, to be used for the memorial to his former commander-in-chief. The hill, (then called Howard's Woods), considered for the monument, was far from any homes and a safe distance from what was then the city. On July 4, 1815, the cornerstone was placed

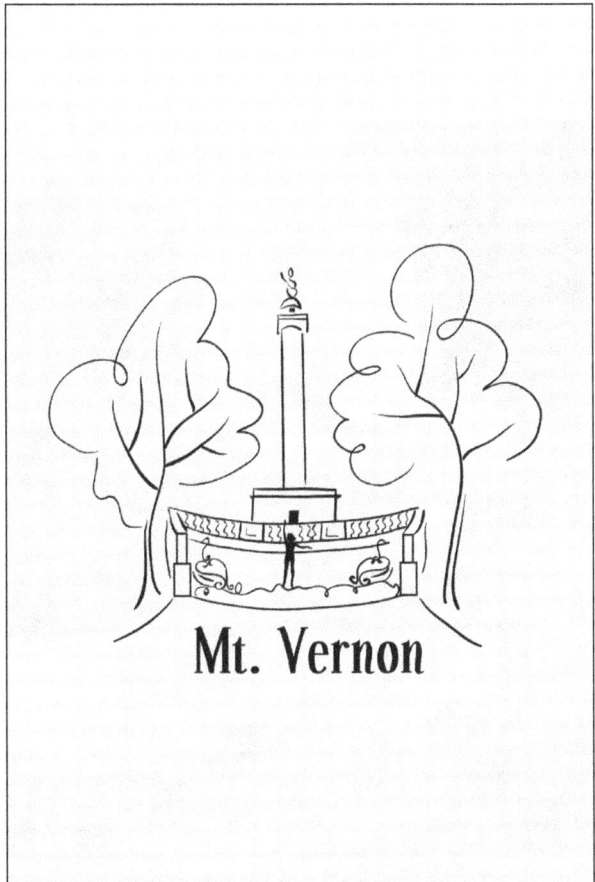

Mt. Vernon

and the construction began. In November 1829, thousands and thousands of dollars over budget, the statue was completed. Colonel Howard was not there to see this event. He had died in 1827. His heirs, however, are given credit for the beautiful Greek Cross design that makes up the four park squares. The squares running north-south are called Washington Place. The squares running east-west are called Mt. Vernon Place, although Mt. Vernon now refers to the surrounding neighborhood.

By the 1840s Baltimore grew and the monument was no longer in the woods. Howard's heirs sold off land around the squares, and in 1842 William Tiffany built what is known as the Tiffany-Fisher House at Eight West Mt. Vernon Place. The Walters Art Gallery Asian Collection and the Engineering Society both occupy prominent 19th-century Mt. Vernon mansions on the square. When the Walters Collection became too large for the house, Henry Walters commissioned the building of a new space. Walters, who died in 1931, left his collection to the City of Baltimore. Between 1858 and 1878 the Peabody Institute was built and expanded at One East Mt. Vernon Place. The Methodist church gives the place the feel of old Vienna. By the 1850s the area was growing into the elite neighborhood that it would become. By the 1890s the sculpture garden was being created and remains today.

This view is looking west from the monument in the early 20th century.

102

This is the west square, *c.* 1914. (Courtesy of Enoch Pratt Free Library.)

This etching by Anton Schutz looks east toward the monument. (Courtesy of Enoch Pratt Free Library.)

This same view of the monument also shows the elms and Japanese cherry trees, 1938. (Courtesy of Enoch Pratt Free Library.)

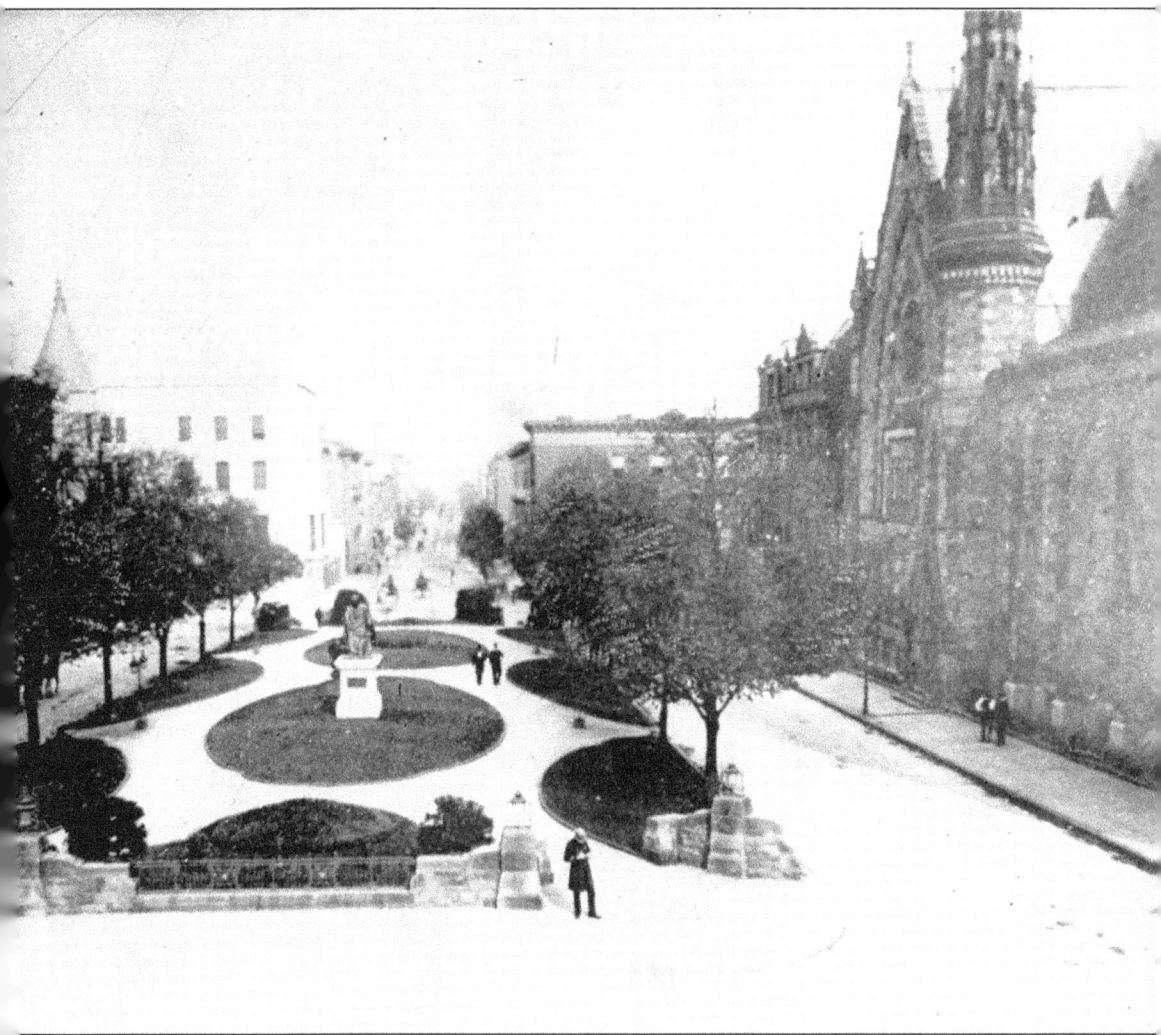

This photo offers another incarnation of the landscape of Mt. Vernon, c. 1895. (Courtesy of Enoch Pratt Free Library.)

This view (left) is from the south square, *c.* 1910. In the etching below by Gabrielle De V. Clements, we have the same view in 1925. (Courtesy of Enoch Pratt Free Library.)

This is a modern view from the south square. (Photo by Peggy Fussell.)

This 1968 postcard is of the 50th annual Flower Mart, traditionally held the second Wednesday of May at the base of the monument. (Courtesy of Gerald Moudry's postcard collection, Cylburn Arboretum.)

A crowd gathers at Lafayette Monument dedication ceremony, September 6, 1924. President Coolidge made the address when it was unveiled. (Courtesy of Enoch Pratt Free Library.)

This photograph of the City Highway Engineer Department truck was taken at the monument, in 1916. (Courtesy of Enoch Pratt Free Library.)

Ten

GWYNNS FALLS
LEAKIN PARK

Gwynns Falls/Leakin Park was another Olmsted brothers vision. In their 1904 Plan, they had hoped to protect it from future development. The land constitutes one of the largest municipal tracts in the United States and is home to one of the most significant urban forests in the country. In 1991 the Department of Recreation and Parks completed a Strategic Plan for Action, and support from non-profit partners, the State, and city agencies helped breath new life into the idea of a linear park system connecting several neighborhood or multi-purpose parks to each other. The 1991 action plan further incorporated issues such as ecological concerns and social justice regarding access to recreational opportunities. Trust for Public Land, a national land conservation organization, recently completed a 10-year process to acquire 11 properties needed to link

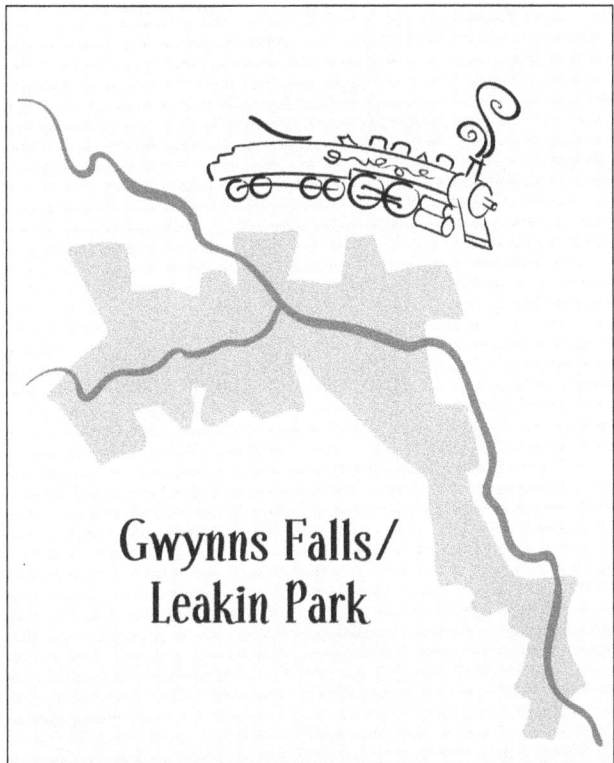

Gwynns Falls/
Leakin Park

and connect existing park land to each other for the Gwynns Falls Trail, a process that represents a partial fulfillment of the Olmstead recommendations. The Stream Valley—stretching from Gwynns Falls/Leakin Park in the north and Middle Branch Park and the Inner Harbor to the South—is calculated at over 2,000 acres of parkland on the westside. Like the Jones Falls, Gwynns Falls powered mills. Gwynns Falls Park was established in 1908. The Gwynns Falls Stream Valley is home to Gwynns Falls Park, to which Leakin Park and the historic Crimea Mansion were added in between 1941 and 1948, when the City acquired land using money left by John Wilson Leakin.

Gwynns Falls/Leakin Park is also home to the Crimea Mansion, located off of Windsor Mill Road. This was the country estate established in the mid-19th century by Thomas Winans, son of B&O locomotive designer and industrialist Ross Winans. After returning from work helping build the St. Petersburg to Moscow Railroad in Russia, Thomas erected the Crimea. The Crimea, completed in 1856–1857, was constructed along with other outbuildings such as a root cellar, smoke house, mock fort, and wooden chapel. The mansion, which sits on a hill, was supplied water from the valley area below. This area has now been aptly renamed Winan's Meadow, home to the picnic pavilion, amphitheater, and the first phase of the Gwynns Falls Trail. The Chesapeake & Allegheny Steam Preservation Society provides a small scale passenger railroad station and tracks for pleasure rides off of the main entrance to the Crimea Mansion. Also located off Windsor Mill is the Carrie Murray Center. Owned by the Department of Recreation and Parks, the center operates a rehabilitation facility for permanently injured birds of prey as well as a display of reptiles. The center was established by a gift from Eddie Murray, former Baltimore Oriole, in honor of his mother, to provide environmental education in Baltimore City.

Archaeological reports from the Baltimore City Center for Urban Archaeology and the Maryland State Historical Trust suggest a high probability of Native American presence in the Gwynns Falls Valley. There are strong indications that the Seneca or Susquehanock Indians traveling from Pennsylvania to areas of Southern Maryland crossed the Gwynns Falls.

– with Halle Van der Gaag of the Trust for Public Land

This 1899 photo shows some young people fishing in the Gwynns Falls. Considered "Baltimore's Niagara Falls," Gwynns Falls once had a dam south of Edmondson Avenue before the turn of the century. (Courtesy of Enoch Pratt Free Library.)

Two men and a dog are shown near Edmonson Avenue Bridge in 1907.

A view captured Gwynns Falls, c. 1912. (Courtesy of Enoch Pratt Free Library.)

This stream is near Dickeyville (Hillsdale), pictured in April 1907.

North of the Edmondson Bridge, this man and woman are sitting on what was known as "Lover's Rock." (Courtesy of Enoch Pratt Free Library.)

113

This is an old mill site on the stream, pictured in 1907.

Gwynns Falls Bridge is captured *c.* 1900. (Courtesy of Enoch Pratt Free Library.)

Eleven

WYMAN PARK

Designed and built as a naturalized public park space in 1911–1914, Wyman Park (bounded by scenic San Martin Drive and Wyman Park Dell) are Baltimore's best remaining examples of a fully-realized park design by the esteemed Olmsted brothers' firm of Brookline, Massachusetts. The 1904 Olmsted brothers plan for The Development of Public Grounds for Great Baltimore envisioned Wyman Park to link the existing large parks—Carroll Park, Druid Hill Park, Clifton, and Patterson Park—into a system of parks and boulevards to break the monotony of the city's grid, then pushing outward at a dramatic pace.

The linear Wyman Park is defined by the dramatic topography of the Stoney Run Valley, a tributary of the Jones Falls. Abandoned in 1943, the Maryland & Pennsylvania Rail Road carried passengers north through fragments of the native beech woodlands. Today the Jones Falls Watershed Association is working on the restoration of the stream's buffers and major public improvements for water quality throughout the valley. Wyman Park Dell is

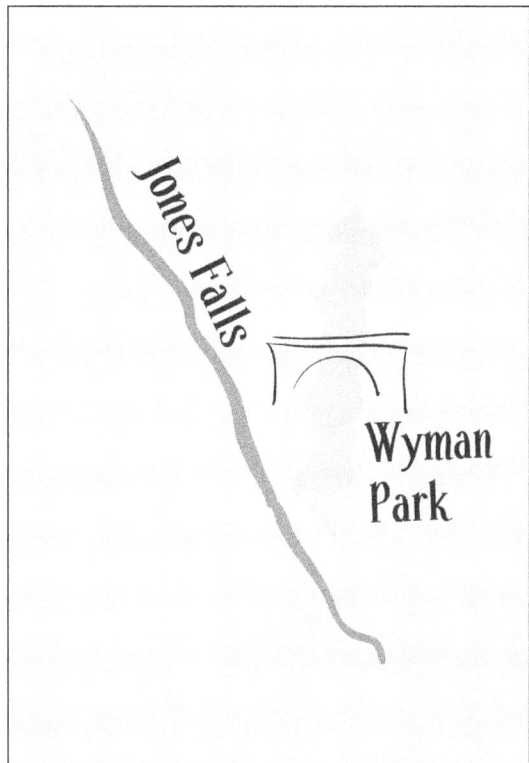

a naturalized landscape built over Sumwalt's Run, which still flows through a massive buried culvert into Stoney Run.

The Olmsted firm carefully planned the new Johns Hopkins University Homewood Campus for the estate of William Wyman, who had bequeathed the remainder as Wyman Park to Baltimore City in 1902. In the 1920s the Olmsted firm successfully recommended the site for building the Baltimore Museum of Art to overlook Wyman Park Dell, for which Johns Hopkins University contributed seven acres of its adjoining campus.

In 1961 Hopkins bought 30 acres of Wyman Park to expand the Homewood Campus along Stoney Run. The City sold the Boy Scouts of America 10 acres in 1968 for its headquarters at the western end of Wyman Park by the Jones Falls. In 2004 the new Jones Falls Trail rises from the Jones Falls Valley for a trailhead with a parking lot at the Steiff Building opposite the Boy Scouts.

Starting in 1997 the Charles Village Festival on the first weekend in June has attracted thousands to Wyman Park Dell. Since 1983 the Friends of Wyman Park Dell, Inc., has served as steward for the largest green space in Charles Village. Strong support for the larger and more natural Wyman Park comes from the Hampden, Keswick, Remington, Stone Hill, and Wyman Park communities to the north and west.

–Sandra R. Sparks, President Emeritus, Friends of Maryland's Olmsted Parks & Landscapes, Inc.

Wyman Park is shown in the winter. This 1935 photograph by W.R. Culver shows sledding and fun in the snow. (Courtesy of the Enoch Pratt Free Library.)

This photo shows a large-scale grading project in Wyman Park, *c.* 1912. (Courtesy of Enoch Pratt Free Library.)

Above is a view from the road behind Homewood Campus in 1941, and below it is seen c. 1940. (Courtesy of Enoch Pratt Free Library.)

As we can see from these 2004 photographs, Wyman Park today is as lovely as ever. (Photographs by Nathaniel Unger Bowditch.)

These photographs taken in 2004 show some of Wyman Park's open spaces. (Photographs by Nathaniel Unger Bowditch.)

Twelve

BALTIMORE'S OTHER
RESPLENDENT TREASURES

In a city where there are squares, gardens, and small parks, a book that covered every green space would be a tome indeed. Other historic parks and gardens include Broadway squares, Franklin Square, Lafayette Square, Linkwood, Mt. Royal Terrace, Roosevelt Park, Fort Armistead, Hanlon Park, Madison Square, Middle Branch and Reedbird Parks, and Union Square, as well as Moores Run, Chinquapin Run Park, and Mt. Pleasant. Seven of the parks have urban farming: Patterson, Clifton, Druid Hill, Carroll, Gwynns Falls/Leakin (all included in this book), DeWees, and Fort Holabird. Gardens no longer around, like Johnston Square and Collington Square (now both sites for schools), should also be noted. Places like Robert E. Lee Park and other parks that are just outside of the city limits were not included for that fact alone. They are still fabulous places to explore. Newer parks like Canton Waterfront Park are not considered historic and were also omitted. In this chapter we will explore some of the beautiful spaces and historic photos of other lovely gardens and parks in Baltimore City.

Baltimore's
Other Resplendent Treasures

Located in Bolton Hill, Eutaw Place is named after the heroic victory by Baltimore's own John Eagar Howard in 1781 at the Revolutionary War Battle of Eutaw Springs. In 1853 Henry Tiffany donated land to develop broad promenades at the street's center as in many European cities. These public squares extend several blocks and are festooned with fountains, gardens, and large metal urns dripping with vines and coleus. This photograph was taken by the Baltimore Camera Club in 1890. (Courtesy of Enoch Pratt Free Library; caption by Tim Almaguer.)

Perkins Spring Square is a post–Civil War park formed from acreage of Chatsworth estate. Perkins Square is a small (1.2 acres) triangular park that was created after the early residents petitioned the City for its creation in 1872. The City leased the land from its owner, Dr. Joseph Perkins. A city gardener maintained the square's landscape with flowers from a nearby greenhouse, and a freshwater spring produced water of supposed "medicinal" quality. The spring is covered with a Victorian Moorish–styled iron pavilion. (Courtesy of The Friends of Patterson Park; caption by Tim Almaguer.)

This painting of Harlem Park by Nicolino Calyo (an Italian painter listed in the Baltimore Directory in 1835) was done between 1830 and 1840. It depicts Harlem (also spelled "Haerlem" or "Haarlem"), which was the home of Dr. Thomas Edmondson. In 1868 the land was given to the City by the Edmondson estate and became Harlem Park. The house in the distance is believed to be Mt. Clare. (Courtesy of Enoch Pratt Free Library.)

Evergreen House is one of Johns Hopkins University's historic houses. It sits on 26 acres and has extensive floral and sculpture gardens, an art gallery, and a museum. The house, built in 1857 by the Broadbent family, became the home of T. Harrison Garrett and his wife, Alice Whitridge Garrett. It was purchased for them by his father, John W. Garrett, president of the Baltimore and Ohio Railroad, in 1878. In 1920 John Work Garrett, son of T. Harrison, inherited the house, where he lived with his wife, Alice Warder Garrett, until his death in 1942. (Courtesy of Enoch Pratt Free Library.)

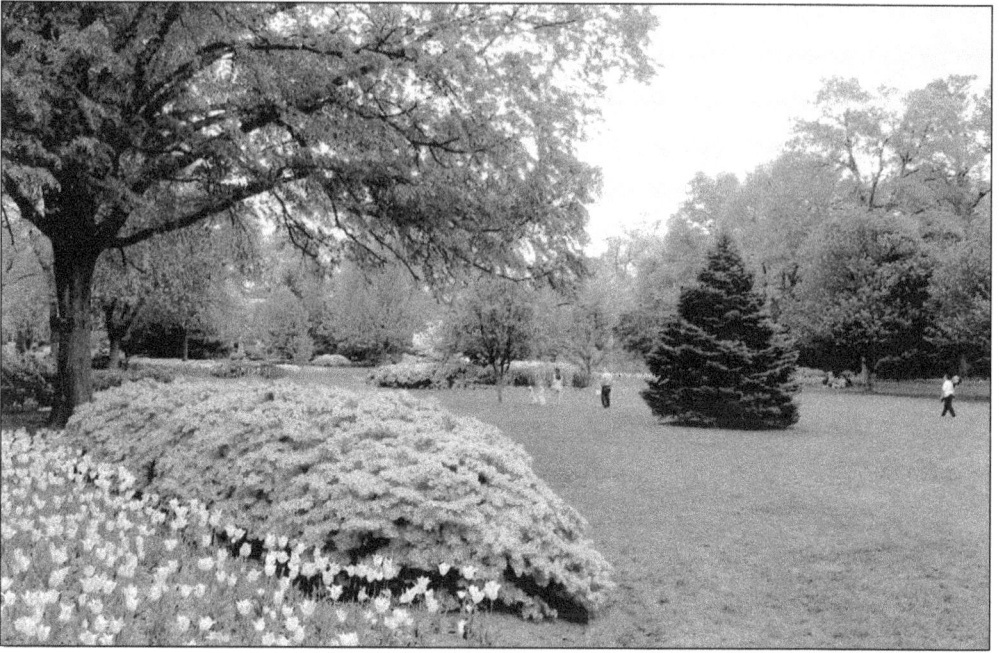

Located in Guilford, Sherwood Gardens was once part of the estate of John Sherwood. He began the garden in 1927, and, even when it was his private land, he allowed garden lovers to stroll through the grounds and admire the beautiful garden behind his mansion. Upon Sherwood's death in 1965, the Guilford Association bought a large portion of the Sherwood Estate so that the gardens could continue. Although the gardens are privately owned, in the spirit of John Sherwood, the public is welcome. (Photo by Nathaniel Unger Bowditch.)

Once known as Battery Park for its role in the War of 1812 (as the site of the "Six-Gun Battery"), it was renamed Riverside Park in 1873. Overlooking the Patapsco River, the park had been planned as a leisure walking and relaxing area. This Riverside Park postcard dates to 1900. (Courtesy of Gerald Moudry's postcard collection, Cylburn Arboretum.)

Preston Gardens is shown here. Mayor James H. Preston hired Thomas Hastings in 1917 to design the park. The original plan was to dedicate it to the mayor's friend, Cardinal Gibbons, and shape the space into a Roman cross. This idea was rejected. The first dedication of the gardens, then called Preston Terraces, was in 1919. In the 1950s the park's flowers were arranged as a "floral calendar," and the day, month, and year were spelled out in flowers daily. (Courtesy of Enoch Pratt Free Library.)

Like Gwynns Falls and other mill streams, Jones Falls has been less than pristine and suffered contamination and pollution for well over 200 years. In 1914, the year an ordinance was passed to create what is now Preston Gardens, the Fallsway was sealed because of the horrendous state of the water in the city. Another blow to its beauty came during the Works Progress Administration during the 1930s, when many of its banks were altered and cemented. Then in the 1960s the Jones Falls Expressway was built following much of its path. Still breathtaking in many places, the Jones Falls is now used for annual kayak races and other water activities. (Courtesy of Enoch Pratt Free Library.)

ASSOCIATIONS AND ORGANIZATIONS

I. PARK FRIENDS AND GARDEN ORGANIZATIONS

Baltimore Alliance for Great
Urban Parks
(410) 243-2156

Baltimore Conservatory
Association
(410) 396-1008

Carroll Park Restoration
Foundation, Inc.
(410) 323-5236

Cylburn Arboretum
Association
(410) 367-2217
www.CylburnAssociation.org

Federated Garden Clubs of
Maryland
(410) 785-2068

Flower Mart at Mt. Vernon,
Ltd.
(410) 539-5855

Friends of Gwynns Falls/Leakin
Park
www.leakinpark.com

Friends of Mt. Vernon Place
(443) 524-2370
www.teammetrix.com/fmvp/

Friends of Maryland's Olmsted
Parks and Landscapes
(410) 323-6690

Friends of Patterson Park
(410) 276-3676
www.pattersonpark.com

Greater Baltimore Master
Gardeners Association
Maryland Cooperative
Extension Service
(Baltimore City Office)
(410) 396-1888

Harlem Park Revitalization
Corporation
(410) 728-5086

Parks and People Foundation
(410) 448-5663
www.parksandpeople.org

Woodberry Land Trust, Inc.
(410) 367-8855

Stratford Green, Inc.
(410) 366-2672

II. CULTURAL AND HISTORICAL ORGANIZATIONS

Baltimore Architecture
Foundation
410.537.7772
www.baltimorearchitecture.org

Baltimore City Heritage Area
www.ci.baltimore.md.us/
government/heritage

Baltimore Heritage, Inc.
(410) 332-9992
www.baltimoreheritage.org

Clifton Mansion/Civic Works
2701 St. Lo Drive
Baltimore, MD 21213
(410) 366-8533 ext. 203
www.civicworks.com/mansiontext

Enoch Pratt Free Library
Maryland Department
(410) 396-5430
www.pratt.lib.md.us/slrc/md/
Evergreen House Foundation,
Inc.
(410) 516-0341
www.jhu.edu/historichouses/

Maryland Historical Society
(410) 685-3750
www.mdhs.org

Maryland Historical Trust
(410) 514-7600
www.marylandhistoricaltrust.net

Preservation Maryland
(410) 685-2886
www.preservemd.org

The Preservation Society
(Federal Hill and Fells Point)
(410) 675-6750
www.preservationsociety.org

III. ENVIRONMENTAL ORGANIZATIONS

Baltimore Bird Club
(800) 823-0050
www.baltimorebirdclub.org

Baltimore/Chesapeake Bay
Outward Bound Program
Communities Organizing to
Revitalize our Environment
(CORE)
(410) 448-1721
www.hurricaneisland.org

Baltimore Ecosystem Study
(410) 455-8011
www.ecostudies.org/BES

Baltimore Harbor Watershed
Association
(410) 563-7300

Gwynns Falls Trail Council
(410) 448-5663 ext. 113
http://www.gwynnsfallstrail.org

Concerned Citizens of
Woodbury
www.aboutwoodberry.com

Gwynns Falls Watershed
Association
(443) 429-3183
www.gwynnsfalls.net

Herring Run Watershed
Association
(410) 254-1577
www.herringrun.org

Irvine Natural Science Center
(Natural Connections)
(410) 484-2413
www.explorenature.com

Jones Falls Watershed
Association
(410) 261-3515
www.jonesfalls.org

Living Classrooms Foundation
(410) 685-0295
www.livingclassrooms.org

Maryland Ornithological
Society
(800) 823-0050
www.mdbirds.org

National Aquarium in
Baltimore
Conservation Education
(410) 576-3800
www.aqua.org/teachandlearn

IV. GOVERNMENT AGENCIES
LOCAL GOVERNMENT

Baltimore City Department of
Planning
http://www.ci.baltimore.md.us

Greenway Trails and Forest
Conservation
(410) 396-8360

Urban Forest/Watersheds/Open
Space
(410) 396-4264

Baltimore City Department of
Recreation and Parks
(410) 396-6132
www.ci.baltimore.md.us

City Forestry
(410) 396-6108

Division of Horticulture
(410) 396-0180

Carrie Murray Nature Center
(410) 396-0808

Gwynns Falls Trail
(410) 396-0440
www.gwynnsfallstrail.org

Baltimore County Department
of Environmental Protection
and Resource Management
Baltimore County Watershed
Management Program
(410) 887-4488

STATE/REGIONAL/NATIONAL ORGANIZATIONS

Alliance for the Chesapeake
Bay
(410) 377-6270
www.AllianceChesBay.org

Center for Watershed
Protection
(410) 461-8323
www.cwp.org

Chesapeake Audubon Society-
Maryland
(410) 822-4903
www.chesapeakeaudubon.org

Chesapeake Bay Foundation
(Maryland State Office)
(410) 269-1870
www.cbf.org

Chesapeake Bay Trust
(410) 974-2941
www.chesapeakebaytrust.org

Department of Natural
Resources Watershed
Protection and Restoration
(410) 260-8810
www.dnr.state.md.us/watersheds

Maryland Environmental Trust
(410) 514-7900
www.dnr.state.md.us/met

Maryland Greenways
Commission
(410) 260-8778
www.dnr.state.md.us/greenways

National Park Service
Rivers, Trails and Conservation
Assistance
The Chesapeake Gateways and
Water Trails Network
(410) 267-5787
www.baygateways.net

1000 Friends of Maryland
(410) 385-2910
www.friendsofmd.org

Tree-Mendous Maryland
(410) 260-8510
www.dnr.state.md.us/treemendous

Trust For Public Land
Baltimore Field Office
(410) 243-3698
www.tpl.org

BIBLIOGRAPHY

Brosius, Myra, Mark Cameron, and Heather Griffing. Discovering Baltimore's Parks, booklet for Conference April 29–May 2, 2000. Baltimore; Presented by Baltimore Alliance for Greater Urban Parks.

Kessler, Barry and David Zang. *The Play Life of a City: Baltimore's Recreation and Parks, 1900–1955*. Baltimore: Baltimore City Life Museums, Baltimore City Department of Recreation and Parks, 1989.

Olmsted Brothers. *Report Upon the Development of Public Grounds for Greater Baltimore*. Baltimore: Lord Baltimore Press, 1904.

Park Commission of the City of Baltimore. *Annual Reports*, 1800s.

Sarudy, Barbara Wells. *Gardens and Gardening in the Chesapeake, 1700–1805*. Baltimore: Johns Hopkins University Press, 1998.